I0139802

SUGGESTIBILITY

Jon Klein

BROADWAY PLAY PUBLISHING INC
224 E 62nd St, NY, NY 10065
www.broadwayplaypub.com
info@broadwayplaypub.com

SUGGESTIBILITY
© Copyright 2007 by Jon Klein

First printing: August 2007
I S B N: 0-88145-340-4

Book design: Marie Donovan
Word processing: Microsoft Word
Typographic controls: Ventura Publisher
Typeface: Palatino
Printed and bound in the U S A

SUGGESTIBILITY opened on 11 March 2006 at the
Victory Theater (Tom Ormeny and Maria Gobetti,
C-Artisitic Directors) in Burbank CA. The cast and
creative contributors were:

CHAD .... John Hansen
SHAWN ....Diane Hudock
KENNETH ....Christopher Rydman
VOICES ..... David Colville, Diane Costa, Brian Haigh
                        & Randi Lynne Weidman

Director .... Maria Gobetti
Set design ....Cynthia Ignacio
Costume design .... Dawn DeWitt

CHARACTERS & SETTING:

KENNETH, *man, around thirty*
SHAWN, *woman, around thirty*
CHAD, *man, around thirty*

There are three settings, requiring minimal furnishings:
A pub interior, with table and chairs
A shared computer station in a brokerage firm
A small den in KENNETH's *home, also equipped with computer*

Sound: There are a number of voiceovers in the course of the play, to suggest participants in internet chat rooms:

Lonely2 *(male)*
2Sexy4U *(female)*
Ursula *(female)*
Monitor *(male)*
Computer voice *(at the end of the play—genderless; effect is robotic)*

for Laura
to whom I suggested marriage

ACT ONE

Scene One

(Lunch at the pub. CHAD *is telling a raunchy story, while* KENNETH *listens politely and* SHAWN *squirms with impatience.)*

CHAD: So the C E O of this Fortune 500 company decides to restructure the chain of command. According to sexual prowess.

SHAWN: Naturally.

CHAD: Since it's his belief that power and authority is reflected by a man's ability to...

SHAWN: Inflate himself?

CHAD: He instructs a doctor to measure the size of each member's...member. And rank them accordingly.

SHAWN: No women work there, I suppose.

CHAD: Not for the purposes of this story.

SHAWN: Of course.

CHAD: Now according to the doctor's findings, the number two job—Senior Vice President—should be occupied by the mail room clerk. A boy of fifteen. Imagine the C E O's surprise. How can a mere boy, without any experience as a power broker, be so heavily endowed?

SHAWN: It boggles the mind.

CHAD: He insists on seeing for himself.

SHAWN: Ah, homoeroticism. A recurring feature of your stories, I've noticed.

CHAD: Do you mind?

SHAWN: Inevitably.

CHAD: So the C E O rounds up the board of directors, and they all head for the mail room to find this extraordinary boy. But on examination, the kid is unimpressive. An average appendage at the least.

SHAWN: Oh, a brain teaser. Or should I say—

CHAD: Moving on. The C E O was worried, but now he's regained his confidence. So he unzips, reveals himself and asks the doctor to record the measurement. But just as the doctor pulls out his calipers, the kid says, oh, by the way, this fax just came in for you. He hands it over to the boss. Turns out it's a new financial report—announcing a hostile takeover of his own company. The stock price has plummeted due to speculation. And rumors say the C E O will be asked to resign by the Board of Directors. Everyone looks down at the boss's...um...

SHAWN: Euphemism—

CHAD: Which has now shrunk to the size of a thimble. So the Board of Directors immediately fires the C E O, and replaces him with the mail room boy. Which proves that the greatest power of all...is the power of suggestion.

(Pause)

KENNETH: This really happened?

CHAD: No, Kenneth. It's a parable. Like the ones in the Bible.

SHAWN: Not exactly.

CHAD: It's about the ephemeral nature of personal security.

SHAWN: It's a penis joke.

CHAD: That too.

KENNETH: I don't get it. How does a mail room boy know about this merger before the head of the company?

CHAD: He doesn't. He made the whole thing up. That's the whole point. See, the kid gave him a bogus report.

KENNETH: You didn't explain that part.

CHAD: What do you want, footnotes?

KENNETH: How else are we supposed to figure it out?

CHAD: She didn't have any trouble. Did you, Shawn?

SHAWN: Only with the inherently offensive sexism.

CHAD: See? She understood it.

KENNETH: I'm just saying it requires a little more information.

CHAD: What it requires is a sense of humor.

SHAWN: Ease up, Chad.

CHAD: How long have you been working here, Kenneth? Six weeks?

KENNETH: Something like that.

CHAD: All that time and I still can't get a handle on you. What *do* you find funny? Or sad? What turns you on? What do you think about? What do you feel? These are easy questions.

SHAWN: You're embarrassing him.

CHAD: At least that would be a response.

KENNETH: Sorry I'm so frustrating.

SHAWN: Believe me, you're not. Chad just believes in grilling newcomers. It's his way of marking territory. Like pissing in a circle.

CHAD: I just want to be friends. That's all. A man can never use too many friends.

KENNETH: I agree.

CHAD: But you make it very difficult. You keep everyone in the office at arm's length.

SHAWN: That's a bit strong.

KENNETH: Surely not the whole arm...maybe up to the elbow...

CHAD: See what I mean? That clever little joke is your way of diverting the truth...when it gets too close.

KENNETH: I know. Look, I know what you...and I do appreciate...believe me, you're not the first person to... I just get...I don't know what...to say.

(Pause)

CHAD: Well, that's a start. Not a very good one, but—

KENNETH: Okay...what do you want to know?

SHAWN: Nothing. He's browbeating you.

CHAD: His brow looks fine to me.

KENNETH: It's all right. I'd like to try. Where do I begin?

CHAD: How about a little personal info. I already checked your job application.

SHAWN: You looked at the H R files? Those are none of your business.

CHAD: I generally *make* it my business. Especially when we hire a new account manager. So tell me more. I know you're not married.

SHAWN: Really? I mean, we all assumed...

CHAD: And you used to handle some very high profile portfolios out on the West Coast—at, what, a third more salary? Now what would lure you to take a pay cut to move across the country and join this podunk outfit?

KENNETH: You make me sound so mysterious.

CHAD: That's because you are. Come on now, spill it. What's your personal life all about? Girlfriend? Boyfriend? Pets? Devoted to a life of monastic deprivation? Addicted to pornography? Any hobbies? Train sets? The race track? New age mysticism? Theoretical physics? Belong to the Sierra Club? Any paramilitary groups? Vampire cults? How about aesthetic preferences? Spielberg or Scorsese? Updike or Grisham? Pepsi or Coke? Diet Pepsi or Diet Coke?

SHAWN: Chad—

CHAD: How personal can a soft drink be?

SHAWN: He's not comfortable.

CHAD: I understand that, but I have a curious nature that cannot be denied. Especially when it comes to people who manage to land corporate accounts in their first six weeks. And the Hawthorne Group at that. Very impressive.

KENNETH: Not at all. I have very little social life, so I throw my energy into work. I prefer it that way.

SHAWN: Why? I mean...if you want to talk about it.

KENNETH: I don't think I can. Not that I don't want to. It's just...I better get back. I'm expecting a call. (*He stands to leave. He turns back to them.*) Sprite.

CHAD: What?

KENNETH: Not Coke or Pepsi. I like Sprite.

CHAD: See, that tells me volumes already.

KENNETH: Good. Thanks for listening. *(He exits.)*

CHAD: What a wiener.

SHAWN: He wants to talk.

CHAD: About what?

SHAWN: Something happened to him. That he can't discuss. It's too difficult.

CHAD: You got all that?

SHAWN: Yes.

CHAD: From what he just said?

SHAWN: From what he *didn't* say.

CHAD: You're interested.

SHAWN: Yes.

CHAD: In him.

SHAWN: Maybe.

CHAD: What for?

SHAWN: I'm intrigued. It's a challenge.

CHAD: Oh, it's a challenge all right. A challenge to find a discernible personality. There's nothing there. The only thing he's trying to hide is how boring he is.

SHAWN: That's your opinion.

CHAD: So this routine works for you? All I ever had to do was mope around like some dyspeptic koala bear? And you'd have gone out with me?

SHAWN: I didn't say I wanted to go out with him.

CHAD: He's a drag.

SHAWN: He's interesting.

CHAD: He's not available. I am.

SHAWN: Oh, right. For one of your famous weekend ski packages.

CHAD: Complete with lift tickets and in-room jacuzzi. The offer still stands.

SHAWN: How much actual skiing is involved?

CHAD: Do you question my intentions?

SHAWN: Daily. *(She stands and hands him the bill.)* Here. It's cheaper than a ski trip. And you still had the pleasure of my company.

(He grabs her hand.)

CHAD: That's all I've ever wanted.

SHAWN: Behave yourself.

CHAD: Tell me how.

SHAWN: By accepting the situation. *(He releases her.)* And don't be stingy. Leave a little something extra behind. *(She exits.)*

CHAD: I always do.

Scene Two

(KENNETH's den at night. He is sitting in his bathrobe, illuminated solely by the light of his computer.)

(He types as he speaks.)

KENNETH: "Hello. Is...anybody...there?"

(He waits for a response. A VOICEOVER is heard over the sound system, as he reads the text on his screen.)

VOICEOVER: *(Lonely2)* Thank God! Human contact! I've been alone in cyberspace for twenty minutes. I thought I'd never connect.

KENNETH: "I...know...what...you...mean."

VOICEOVER: *(Lonely2)* You're up late.

KENNETH: "So...are...you."

VOICEOVER: *(Lonely2)* Can't sleep?

KENNETH: "Not...usually."

VOICEOVER: *(Lonely2)* Me either.

KENNETH: "Why...are...you...Lonely...number...two? Is...there...a...number...one?"

VOICEOVER: *(Lonely2)* No, no. It's Lonely2, not Lonely number 2. Lonely also. Aren't you?

KENNETH: "Not...really."

VOICEOVER: *(Lonely2)* That's your first lie tonight. Is your name really Ishmael? What is it, Jewish?

KENNETH: "It's...from...*Moby...Dick.*"

VOICEOVER: *(Lonely2)* Now you're talking. What do you look like?

KENNETH: "It's...not...important."

VOICEOVER: *(Lonely2)* What, are you kidding?

KENNETH: "I...just...want...a...little...social...intercourse."

VOICEOVER: *(Lonely2)* Me too. Tell me how you like it.

KENNETH: "I'm...looking...for...a...friend."

VOICEOVER: *(Lonely2)* Do you have an unusual fantasy?

KENNETH: "No...I...want...something...real."

VOICEOVER: *(Lonely2)* Do you want to get off?

KENNETH: "I...just...got...on."

VOICEOVER: *(Lonely2)* I can help you feel good. I can make you come.

KENNETH: "Oh...I...see. No...thank...you."

VOICEOVER: *(Lonely2)* What's wrong?

KENNETH: "This...was...a...mistake."

VOICEOVER: *(Lonely2)* Don't go.

KENNETH: "Sorry."

VOICEOVER: *(Lonely2)* Call me, Ishmael.

(KENNETH *pushes a button on the keyboard.)*

KENNETH: Escape.

(He turns off the computer.)

Scene Three

(The office cubicle. SHAWN *is working at the computer while* CHAD *sits on the corner of the desk.)*

CHAD: Friday night.

SHAWN: No.

CHAD: Saturday night.

SHAWN: Why don't you ever take "no" for an answer?

CHAD: "No" isn't an answer. It's a reply. But it doesn't answer anything.

SHAWN: All right, here's your answer. Three answers. One. Because after ten or twenty destructive relationships, I've learned that it would be simpler just to hit myself in the head with the claw end of a hammer. Two. Because I'm apparently looking for a different species of male than the ones found on this particular planet. And three. Because the next time I decide to throw caution to the wind, my very last choice for a date would be a sexually aggressive, verbally abusive, high-maintenance mass of hostility like you.

(Pause)

CHAD: You're secretly attracted to me, aren't you?

SHAWN: I wonder what you're really like, Chad.
Under all the pretense.

CHAD: You think I'm pretending? To be what?

SHAWN: I'm not sure. But I don't think it's human.

CHAD: What would you like me to be?

SHAWN: I'm curious about what makes you so insecure
that you have to overcompensate.

CHAD: What are you talking about? I'm completely
relaxed.

SHAWN: You're as relaxed as a used car dealer.
And about as subtle.

CHAD: Is it wrong to go after the things you want?

SHAWN: In your case, yes.

CHAD: Okay. I'll leave you alone.

SHAWN: No you won't.

CHAD: Why do you hate me?

SHAWN: I don't hate you, Chad. I don't even know you.
You won't allow it. You've got this elaborate charade
of personality all worked out, to take the place of
something more genuine. Something that must scare
you pretty badly. I wonder what it is.

CHAD: I've got nothing to hide.

SHAWN: Of course you do. We all do. But you're hiding
the wrong part. Most people keep their dark and
twisted sides under wraps. Out of sight. Not you.
You push it right up front where everyone gapes at
it in horror.

CHAD: Now you're just insulting me.

SHAWN: I wish I knew whatever caused all this.

CHAD: Whoever.

SHAWN: Whomever. A woman. Of course. What was her name?

CHAD: Let's see. Should I do this alphabetically? There was Alice. And Barbara.

SHAWN: This is a lot of anger for one man to handle.

CHAD: And Cynthia. And Darlene. And Erin. And—

SHAWN: You're actually going to come up with twenty-six.

CHAD: In the first round.

SHAWN: Which one is your mother?

CHAD: They all are. Isn't that what you're thinking?

SHAWN: Didn't occur to me.

CHAD: Tell me something. What qualifies you to judge me?

SHAWN: You're right. I apologize. After all, I have my own list of names.

CHAD: Then why not give me a chance?

SHAWN: Look, Chad. It's one thing to step in front of an approaching train. That's being...oblivious, I guess. Unaware. But to see the train coming first, and then to take the same step—that's either being stupid or suicidal. Either way—no thanks.

CHAD: What if I love you?

(She stifles a laugh.)

SHAWN: Oh, God. And you said you were serious.

CHAD: I am.

SHAWN: Let's not do this, Chad.

CHAD: Do what?

SHAWN: Use words.

CHAD: Words?

SHAWN: Words like "love".

CHAD: It's not just a word.

SHAWN: Yes it is. That's my point exactly. It's *never* more than just a word.

CHAD: And you accuse *me* of being cynical.

SHAWN: Words. Vows of passion, promises of faithfulness, endless proclamations of eternal devotion. Just words. Love is a dead language. Like Latin.

CHAD: So you don't believe in love.

SHAWN: I believe in action. In the form of personal sacrifice. Can you possibly know what that means?

(Pause. She burns her gaze into his face.)

CHAD: I think so.

SHAWN: I don't think you do. You should see the expression on your face right now. Like a cow staring at a passing car.

CHAD: Then explain.

SHAWN: Maybe later.

(She sees KENNETH *approaching.)*

SHAWN: Congratulations.

KENNETH: Thank you.

CHAD: What's this about?

KENNETH: It's nothing.

SHAWN: That's not what they said at the sales meeting.

CHAD: What sales meeting?

SHAWN: You had a doctor's appointment. Or said you did.

CHAD: Dentist?

SHAWN: Podiatrist.

CHAD: Damn it. I've been using Ora-Gel when I should be limping.

SHAWN: Like anyone cares enough to notice. Just tell him what happened, Kenneth.

KENNETH: I put together a package. No big deal.

SHAWN: For Mrs. Wharton.

CHAD: Jane Wharton? The heiress?

SHAWN: That's the one.

CHAD: She's been keeping us at bay for years. No one could get her to sign.

KENNETH: So I was told.

CHAD: And you reeled her in. When all others failed.

SHAWN: It's a stunning achievement, Kenneth.

CHAD: What convinced her?

KENNETH: It's a decent plan. She'll do well.

CHAD: Bullshit. That never mattered before. You must have some kind of magic formula for rich, eccentric widows.

KENNETH: I wish.

CHAD: Keeping it to yourself, eh? Is that in the company's interest?

SHAWN: Since when have you cared about that?

CHAD: What are those sales meetings for, anyway? To share successful techniques with the sales staff. Am I right?

SHAWN: For those who bother to attend.

CHAD: Aw, come on. Have a little sympathy. I was having a tooth pulled.

SHAWN: Toe.

CHAD: Toe pulled. Or whatever they do to toes. Just be a team player and share the wealth. What convinced Old Lady Wharton? How'd you get your foot in the door?

KENNETH: Religion.

SHAWN: Come again?

KENNETH: Turns out she's a very religious person. I don't think any of the other account reps took that into...account.

CHAD: How'd you discover this? Pictures of bleeding martyrs on her walls?

KENNETH: Oh no. I've never been to her house. I've never even met her.

CHAD: You put together a brand new portfolio without even meeting her?

KENNETH: I don't do as well in person. Too self-conscious. I'm more confident over the phone. Or fax or E-Mail. That way I can keep a little distance.

SHAWN: How did religion come up?

KENNETH: Just something in the tone of her voice. I could tell she was having difficulty with the moral aspects of speculation. In her mind, investing was a little like casino gambling.

SHAWN: Which it is.

KENNETH: So I thought to myself, what would preoccupy an aging fundamentalist? Guilt.

CHAD: Guilt?

KENNETH: I asked her whether she thought it would be sinful to invest her money. She said maybe.

SHAWN: Good God.

CHAD: What did you say?

KENNETH: I said that I believe human beings are defined by our guilt. And the more forgiveness we require...the more human we become.

SHAWN: Even Chad?

CHAD: Wait a minute. You gave her this...discount theology...and she suddenly decided to sign?

SHAWN: To the tune of twenty million dollars.

KENNETH: Investments are like the afterlife. Uncertain, but comforting.

SHAWN: I've heard some sales pitches before, but guilt...how'd you come up with it?

KENNETH: Oh, I'm an expert on the subject.

SHAWN: How so?

KENNETH: I'm not comfortable...talking about that.

(Pause)

CHAD: Christ, what'd you do, kill somebody?

SHAWN: Stop prying, Chad.

CHAD: I can't help it. I must have pitched to that geriatric crone half a dozen times myself. And the Hawthorne Group before that. What's your secret, Kenneth?

KENNETH: Like I said. It's nothing.

CHAD: Twenty million dollars worth of nothing.

SHAWN: Would you mind giving us a minute, Chad?

CHAD: Huh?

SHAWN: I want to talk to Kenneth.

CHAD: That's what we're doing.

SHAWN: By myself.

CHAD: What for?

SHAWN: It's private.

CHAD: Private.

SHAWN: Yes. Do you mind?

CHAD: You want to be alone with Kenneth.

SHAWN: That's what I said.

CHAD: You and him—alone.

SHAWN: Just get the fuck out of here.

(Pause)

CHAD: Sure. I can take a hint. *(He reluctantly exits.)*

SHAWN: He's intimidated by you. That's all. Don't take it personally.

KENNETH: Intimidated?

SHAWN: By your success. You're a rising star around here, Kenneth. Management thinks highly of you.

KENNETH: That's good to know.

SHAWN: And so...do I.

KENNETH: Well now...I'm sure I don't deserve that.

SHAWN: You take compliments very badly.

KENNETH: I know. One of my many failings.

SHAWN: That's another thing. The way you constantly put yourself down. You have a problem with self-esteem, don't you?

KENNETH: I have a lot of problems. But you don't want to hear about them.

SHAWN: How do you know?

KENNETH: Why would you?

SHAWN: Maybe the chance to get to know you a little better.

KENNETH: Well ...

SHAWN: I'm attracted to you, all right? There. I said it.

KENNETH: Oh. Um...

SHAWN: I'm being too forward.

KENNETH: No.

SHAWN: Now you're scared of me.

KENNETH: Not at all.

SHAWN: But sometimes one person or the other has to jump in and make the first move. Otherwise...nothing happens.

KENNETH: Nothing *will* happen. *(Pause)* I mean... nothing can happen. It's just not...a possibility.

SHAWN: Oh shit. My "Gaydar" is on the fritz again.

KENNETH: It's not that. I like women.

SHAWN: You just don't like me.

KENNETH: Not at all. I mean...yes. Yes I do. Very much.

SHAWN: You have a strange way of expressing it.

KENNETH: It's just...not a good idea. Not because of you. Because of me. It's nothing personal.

(Pause)

SHAWN: Is that all?

KENNETH: I...cause damage.

SHAWN: Damage.

KENNETH: Yes.

SHAWN: How so?

KENNETH: Please...Shawn. This is difficult.

SHAWN: So what? I just put myself on the line. That's not easy for me, you know. You think I throw myself at every man who comes along?

KENNETH: Of course not.

SHAWN: Then if you're going to reject me—I insist on a decent reason.

(Pause)

KENNETH: There is...someone.

SHAWN: Someone. Someone else.

KENNETH: Yes. Someone special.

SHAWN: Out west?

KENNETH: She's the reason...I'm here.

SHAWN: So you're seeing someone else. Why didn't you just ...

KENNETH: No! That's not it. I've never even...I've never even met her. In person.

SHAWN: But she exists, right?

KENNETH: Of course...sort of.

SHAWN: She's not an *imaginary* friend, is she, Kenneth? Maybe with long ears and a puffy tail?

KENNETH: No. She's real.

SHAWN: And she is... *(Pause)* That's your cue to reply, Kenneth. Your what? Your lover, your ex-wife, your sister, your mother, your guardian angel, your psychic friend, your what?

KENNETH: I'm not comfortable discussing this.

SHAWN: Who gives a shit? We crossed that line ten minutes ago, pal. You will tell me what I want to know. Otherwise I will choose to be insulted. And you don't want to see the results of that, believe me. A plague of locusts pales in comparison.

(KENNETH *manages to smile.*)

KENNETH: What do you suggest?

SHAWN: Dinner. On me. In a neutral setting. The Pub. I'll ply you with food and alcohol until your tongue loosens.

KENNETH: Should I be scared?

SHAWN: The procedure will be relatively painless. Unless you struggle.

KENNETH: All right. I give in.

SHAWN: It's after six. Let's do it now.

KENNETH: Just let me check my e-mail.

SHAWN: Be my guest.

(*She rises and lets him sit down at the desk.* KENNETH *pulls up a screen on the computer while she primps.*)

(*We hear a sound on the computer indicating new e-mail.*)

(*He clicks on the mouse.*)

KENNETH: Shit. The Hawthorne Group.

SHAWN: Trouble?

KENNETH: They're just nervous. Always questioning the performance on one or two blue chips. I'd better call them from my desk. Why don't I meet you there at seven?

SHAWN: On the dot. Or else I'll come looking for you.

(*They both exit, in different directions.*)

(CHAD *enters from around the wall of the cubicle, watching them go.*)

(*He sits at the terminal and reads* KENNETH's *e-mail message.*)

CHAD: Careless. Very careless. No telling who could come along and read this. Or even worse... (*He looks around to make sure he's in the clear, then punches the keyboard.*) Print.

Scene Four

(*The pub.* SHAWN *sips on a drink at the table, waiting for* KENNETH. CHAD *enters and sits down across from her.*)

SHAWN: I'm expecting someone.

CHAD: And here I am.

SHAWN: Let's not play games, Chad.

CHAD: All right.

SHAWN: I'm having dinner with Kenneth.

CHAD: Good for you.

SHAWN: I don't know him very well. But yes, I'm interested. I'm hoping to have a nice dinner, and get to know him a little better.

CHAD: How long will this take?

SHAWN: What? Dinner?

CHAD: To get to know him.

SHAWN: I don't know.

CHAD: An hour? A week? A month? A year?

SHAWN: I have no preconceptions.

CHAD: Sure you do. I can see it in your eyes. You already have hope. You're hoping to scrape up enough chit-chat and background info to justify your lustful desires.

SHAWN: You now have my permission to fuck off.

CHAD: I'm worried about you, Shawn. You're going about this a little backwards, aren't you? Shouldn't love begin with friendship?

SHAWN: I'm hoping that will happen.

CHAD: It's too late. You've already got the hots for him. And wondering about the outcome—his place or yours? Be honest with yourself. It's already about sex. Without knowing the first thing about him.

SHAWN: Which is why I suggested dinner. He's a very private man. He needs encouragement.

CHAD: Maybe he's just got nothing to say.

SHAWN: He's in a lot of pain, Chad.

CHAD: So who are you, Florence fucking Nightingale?

SHAWN: He needs someone. To pull him out of himself.

CHAD: What for? For all you know, he's perfectly content in the wonderful world of Kenneth. Alone in his castle. Where the palm fronds obscure the windows just enough for him to peek through, but no one else can see in. He's happy right where he is.

SHAWN: He's lonely.

CHAD: Since when does that concern you? You never came to my rescue.

SHAWN: Look, Chad. Do you know what the ultimate waste of time is? Unrequited love. Or in your case, lust. Get over it already. There are more productive ways to get what you're looking for.

CHAD: What I'm looking for is right here.

SHAWN: See what I mean? Be a little less direct.
It's nauseating.

CHAD: You think I'm too honest.

SHAWN: Overbearing. You should hang back a little.
Have an air of mystery. Don't be so easy to read.

CHAD: Fine. If inaccessibility is what fascinates you,
I'll start studying for the priesthood.

SHAWN: Not necessary. Though a vow of silence might
score some points.

CHAD: Whatever it takes.

SHAWN: All right, Chad. You really want to help me?

CHAD: Yes.

SHAWN: Then let me do this. Let me have time alone
with Kenneth. I will be very appreciative.

CHAD: How appreciative?

SHAWN: I will be your friend.

CHAD: Will you confide in me? So that I'll know where
I stand?

SHAWN: Yes.

CHAD: My...special friend?

SHAWN: Without the lewd connotations currently
passing through your diseased imagination.

CHAD: Damn.

SHAWN: Can you live with that, Chad? I don't want to
cause you pain. But I need to be clear. Am I being clear?

CHAD: Brutally.

SHAWN: That's how you're taking it. That's not my
intention.

CHAD: I want friendship. Not pity.

SHAWN: Glad to hear it.

CHAD: Well...maybe occasional pity.

SHAWN: We'll play it by ear. Shake?

(CHAD *hesitates, then shakes her hand.*)

SHAWN: I'm very pleased about this, Chad.

CHAD: I'm happy if you're happy.

SHAWN: Let's toast to a new start. (*She raises her glass.*)

CHAD: I don't have a drink.

SHAWN: Here he comes. Make yourself scarce.

(KENNETH *enters and takes a chair at the table.*)

KENNETH: Chad! How's it hanging?

CHAD: Never has, never will.

KENNETH: Will you be joining us?

CHAD: No can do, I'm afraid. Not all of us can rest our laurels on twenty million dollar accounts.

(SHAWN *clears her throat disapprovingly.*)

CHAD: Which is why I might come over to your desk tomorrow. If you have the time. I'd love to get a few tips on updating some old portfolios—

KENNETH: I don't know how much I could tell you—

CHAD: If you're too busy—

KENNETH: Not at all. Come by tomorrow.

SHAWN: Good night, Chad.

KENNETH: Sure you can't stay? Shawn wants to get me drunk and make me spill my darkest secrets.

CHAD: Be strong, young warrior. Don't give in to the Dark Force.

SHAWN: Good*bye*, Chad.

CHAD: Right. *(He looks at* SHAWN.*)* See you tomorrow. *(He exits.)*

KENNETH: Is there...pardon me if I'm getting too personal...

SHAWN: Feel free. That's the whole point of this.

KENNETH: You and Chad...

SHAWN: What?

KENNETH: He seems very...interested.

SHAWN: Oh.

KENNETH: In you.

SHAWN: Chad and I have a long-standing...I hesitate to call it a relationship...more of a...codependent revulsion.

KENNETH: I...see.

SHAWN: Sorry. I don't mean to be obtuse. Or to be so obtuse as to use words like "obtuse".

KENNETH: So you and Chad...

SHAWN: Are just friends. Not to worry.

KENNETH: You're sure about his end of it? Maybe he's just reluctant to tell you his feelings.

SHAWN: That will be the day.

KENNETH: Sometimes it's hard to know what's going on.

SHAWN: Then allow me to be straightforward. *(She leans over and kisses him lightly on the lips.)* Or maybe just forward...

KENNETH: Whichever it was...it was very nice.

SHAWN: Thank you. There are many variations.

KENNETH: It's just...I'm not a good candidate for this.

SHAWN: This? What do you call this?

KENNETH: Whatever you...think this is.

SHAWN: Well, so far...not much.

KENNETH: I'm sorry.

SHAWN: So what's the problem? You're not attracted to me?

KENNETH: God, yes. You're an extremely beautiful woman. Way out of my league.

SHAWN: I intimidate you?

KENNETH: Not at all.

SHAWN: I bore you?

KENNETH: Please—it's not you at all. It's me.

SHAWN: So it's the other woman.

KENNETH: No.

SHAWN: Assuming she *is* a woman.

KENNETH: She said she was.

SHAWN: *Said* she was? What does that mean? She's a transsexual?

KENNETH: Please. Let me explain. *(He takes a sip from her drink, then hands it back to her.)* Here's the problem— I don't know what love is.

SHAWN: So fucking what? Neither do I. No one does. Welcome to the human race.

KENNETH: But you know what it feels like.

SHAWN: Well, yeah. I've been there once or twice.

KENNETH: I never have.

SHAWN: Oh. Well, there are many kinds of love, Kenneth. It doesn't always have to be romantic. How about your parents?

KENNETH: Oh, they went through the motions,
I suppose. But they really didn't notice I was there,
most of the time.

SHAWN: It might have felt that way—

KENNETH: No. It *was* that way. So I made up imaginary
creatures. Monsters. Pirates. Alternate parents. They
were easier to talk to.

SHAWN: You were just lonely. And longing for love.

KENNETH: See, that makes no sense to me. It's like
longing for Thai food when you've never tasted it.
I was like some kind of jungle boy, raised by wolves.

SHAWN: Actually, wolves are very affectionate.

KENNETH: Really. I didn't know that. Where was I?

SHAWN: In the jungle.

KENNETH: Oh, right. Childhood. Then high school.
Where I watched everyone go through their first
romances, crushes and heartbreaks. From the outside.
Like some...cultural anthropologist.

SHAWN: Big deal. You managed to avoid the worst part
of adolescence. You were lucky.

KENNETH: I didn't feel lucky. I felt stupid. So I started
reading up on the subject.

SHAWN: What subject? You mean—

KENNETH: This thing called love. I went on a
self-taught, remedial course. I read Keats, Shelley,
Byron, all the Romantic poets. Shakespeare, Plato,
Kierkegaard, Leo Buscaglia. Romantic films—
Casablanca, Wuthering Heights, Love Story. My favorite
was *Vertigo.*

SHAWN: *Vertigo?* That's a little unhealthy, don't you
think?

KENNETH: I couldn't make those distinctions. I still couldn't figure out what I was expected to feel. Other than the brief, temporary satisfaction of sexual release. At first I confused *that* for love. I bet you never made *that* mistake.

SHAWN: Well... Hey. We're not here to talk about me.

KENNETH: Then suddenly, without any warning, it happened.

SHAWN: Thank God. I've been waiting for the juicy part.

KENNETH: It's also...the hardest part. How do I explain this to you? You remember how I said I never actually *saw* her? In person?

SHAWN: Yes...

KENNETH: We met on the Internet.

(Pause)

SHAWN: Oh no.

KENNETH: I know how it sounds...

SHAWN: In what, a chat room?

KENNETH: That's out of date. Now it's called "social software."

SHAWN: I can't believe...didn't you *know* any better? Then to trust some...figment of...somebody else's imagination? Do you know how removed that is from reality?

KENNETH: Oh yes. That was the part I liked the most.

SHAWN: Oh my God.

KENNETH: Her moniker was "Ursula." She worked as a waitress in a Bay Area cafe.

SHAWN: How ambitious.

KENNETH: It was a whole new experience for me.
My heart started to beat more quickly just by turning
on the computer. I couldn't wait to sign on.

SHAWN: With a fantasy!

KENNETH: I know. *(Pause)* Until she made it real.
Too real.

SHAWN: What happened?

KENNETH: She started to suggest we meet in person.

SHAWN: Oh. Well, that's only natural.

KENNETH: Not for me.

SHAWN: Why? Too scared?

KENNETH: No. Too...disappointed. I liked things the
way we were.

SHAWN: Another movie title.

KENNETH: It was never the same after that. And she
could tell how my tone changed. Without ever knowing
why. All she knew was that I seemed more distant—

SHAWN: As though that's even *possible*—

KENNETH: I knew it wasn't real. But I couldn't help it.
I preferred my own version.

SHAWN: The poor girl.

KENNETH: And there it is. Now she's the one who gets
your sympathy. Not me.

SHAWN: Well, I suppose...

KENNETH: See what I mean, Shawn. I'm not the man
for you. It's better to leave me alone. All I do is cause
damage. That's why I quit my job and fled. I had to get
as far away as possible.

SHAWN: But why here?

KENNETH: No particular reason. The furthest location to accept my resume, I suppose.

SHAWN: This is utterly absurd. Don't you ever wonder what would have happened if you met her?

KENNETH: All the time. But it's too late.

SHAWN: It's never too late. It might be worth the try.

KENNETH: I can't. *(Pause)* She's dead.

SHAWN: My God, Kenneth. How do you know?

KENNETH: I killed her. *(He sips on his drink.)*

Scene Five

(The office cubicle. CHAD stares at SHAWN in disbelief.)

CHAD: The guy is a *felon*?

SHAWN: Of course not. He didn't mean it literally.

CHAD: How else do you mean murder?

SHAWN: Figuratively. Sort of. She sent a package to his office building. Containing a copy of *Women In Love*. That's a novel.

CHAD: Thanks. I know D H Lawrence.

SHAWN: Since when?

CHAD: Since high school. I heard it was dirty. What about it?

SHAWN: That's where she got her online name— "Ursula".

CHAD: Hold on. How'd she know *his* name?

SHAWN: She didn't.

CHAD: So how'd she address the package?

SHAWN: With *his* online name. She had no trouble finding him. Evidently it was his nickname around the office.

CHAD: What was it?

SHAWN: The name of a character. From his favorite movie.

CHAD: Let me guess. *Rainman*?

SHAWN: That's not important. Anyway, this book contained a long letter on the last page. Confessing that despite her words to the contrary, she had fallen in love with him.

CHAD: Without ever meeting him. Well, I guess in his case that's an advantage.

SHAWN: And she couldn't imagine life without him.

CHAD: So? Why the weird look? Did I miss something?

SHAWN: He took it literally.

CHAD: Took what? He thought it was a threat?

SHAWN: Maybe.

CHAD: He thinks she killed herself? Over him?

SHAWN: He worries about it, Chad.

CHAD: I've told you the same thing a hundred times.

SHAWN: Yeah. But you never meant it.

CHAD: *Nobody* does. It's just a thing people say.

SHAWN: Kenneth doesn't know that.

CHAD: What's with this guy? Was he raised by wolves?

SHAWN: Funny you should mention that—

CHAD: What an incredible ego.

SHAWN: He went to the café to find her. But she disappeared. He even hired a private detective. Not a trace.

CHAD: Sounds like she had the brains in this relationship.

SHAWN: That's a mean thing to say.

CHAD: Oh, come on, Shawn. So she packed her bags and split. And mailed him a letter guaranteed to make him feel bad. This is unusual behavior? After getting dumped?

SHAWN: Kenneth hasn't had our experience. It's heartbreaking.

CHAD: It's disgusting. He's manipulating you.

SHAWN: Don't talk that way about him.

CHAD: Listen to reason. "My girlfriend killed herself" is the number two ploy for sympathy. Right after "Mommy didn't love me."

SHAWN: This is why I could never see us together, Chad. Your cynicism is overwhelming.

CHAD: All right. Let's assume that Kenneth is one, big, quivering, gelatinous mass of guilt. He thinks he made an old girlfriend bite the big one.

SHAWN: Chad—

CHAD: What really brought him here?

SHAWN: I told you. To get away—

CHAD: Why here exactly? Did he tell you the postmark on her package?

SHAWN: No.

CHAD: I'd ask him.

SHAWN: You think...

CHAD: Just a suggestion.

SHAWN: He followed her here?

CHAD: Who knows? But assuming he's as obsessed as you claim—wouldn't he pursue every clue?

SHAWN: Possibly.

CHAD: I'm just saying be careful. I'm concerned about you.

SHAWN: Thank you, Chad. That means a lot to me.

CHAD: I told you I could be your friend.

SHAWN: Sorry I doubted you.

CHAD: He doesn't want you, Shawn. He's giving you every reason to bail out. And a few he probably hasn't even mentioned yet.

SHAWN: You're right.

CHAD: So you'll give up on him?

SHAWN: Of course not. He needs me more than ever.

CHAD: Excuse me?

SHAWN: This entire story is a cry for help.

CHAD: Perhaps I didn't make myself clear—

SHAWN: No, you were wonderful. It's such a fantastic release to be able to talk about all this. You're the best friend a girl could hope for. *(She rises, kisses him on the cheek and begins to move off.)*

CHAD: Where are you going?

SHAWN: Kenneth and I have a date in an hour. I have to get ready. Wish me luck.

CHAD: Luck...

(She moves off.)

CHAD: Fuck.

Scene Six

(KENNETH's *den. He is in his bathrobe, sitting at his computer. He reads the text on the screen as* VOICEOVERS *converse with him and each other.)*

VOICEOVER: *(2Sexy4U)* So I told him never to call me again.

VOICEOVER: *(Lonely2)* Good for you, ladyfriend. Life's better on the Net anyway.

VOICEOVER: *(2Sexy4U)* Are you there, Ishmael? You're so quiet tonight.

(KENNETH *types as he speaks.)*

KENNETH: "I...have...an...announcement."

VOICEOVER: *(Lonely2)* You're coming out.

KENNETH: "No. Sorry."

VOICEOVER: *(Lonely2)* How disappointing.

VOICEOVER: *(2Sexy4U)* Not to me.

KENNETH: "I'm...saying...goodbye."

VOICEOVER: *(Lonely2)* You're leaving us?

VOICEOVER: *(2Sexy4U)* What about your search for Ursula? We can help you find her.

KENNETH: "No. I...let...her...go. It...was...a...delusion."

VOICEOVER: *(2Sexy4U)* Love is not a delusion.

VOICEOVER: *(Lonely2)* Get with the program, girl.

KENNETH: "Besides. I...need...my...sleep."

VOICEOVER: *(Lonely2)* You know what this sounds like.

VOICEOVER: *(2Sexy4U)* Yes. He's found someone else.

VOICEOVER: *(Lonely2)* Offline.

KENNETH: "Maybe."

VOICEOVER: *(Lonely2)* Don't desert us, Ishmael. Real life isn't what it's cracked up to be.

VOICEOVER: *(2Sexy4U)* Oh, shut up.

VOICEOVER: *(Lonely2)* You shut up.

KENNETH: "Thanks...for...keeping...me...company."

VOICEOVER: *(2Sexy4U)* Good for you, Ishmael. You're the last of the true romantics. We'll miss you.

VOICEOVER: *(Lonely2)* Speak for yourself. There'll be plenty of horny insomniacs to take his place.

VOICEOVER: *(2Sexy4U)* You wish.

VOICEOVER: *(Lonely2)* You wish you had a dick.

VOICEOVER: *(2Sexy4U)* Fuck you.

VOICEOVER: *(Monitor)* Language, folks. Please keep it clean.

VOICEOVER: *(Lonely2)* Quit listening, pervert.

(KENNETH pushes a button on the keyboard.)

KENNETH: Exit.

(SHAWN enters opposite, also dressed in a man's bathrobe. She rubs her eyes.)

SHAWN: Kenneth? What's wrong?

(KENNETH swivels his chair around and takes off the headset.)

KENNETH: Nothing.

SHAWN: Am I interrupting one of your late night gabfests?

KENNETH: I don't...do that anymore. Just checking the market.

SHAWN: It closed eight hours ago.

KENNETH: That's true.

SHAWN: I was afraid of this.

KENNETH: What?

SHAWN: I threw myself at you.

KENNETH: Not at all.

SHAWN: You have second thoughts. We drank too much.

KENNETH: Just a bad habit. Takes a while for me to get sleepy. Nothing to do with you.

SHAWN: How about her?

KENNETH: Who?

SHAWN: You know who. "Ursula." Are you thinking about her?

(Pause)

KENNETH: It will take a little time, Shawn. I'll understand if you don't have the patience.

SHAWN: Can I ask you something? About her?

KENNETH: Anything.

SHAWN: The postmark on her package. Where was it from?

(Pause)

KENNETH: Here. It came from here.

SHAWN: I see.

KENNETH: But she's not here anymore. If she ever was. For all I know it was just a stopover. She wrote it from some motel room on the way to New York, Chicago— Tibet for all I know.

SHAWN: Still—you came here to find her.

KENNETH: Yes. But I gave up weeks ago.

SHAWN: I don't know if I can compete with this memory.

KENNETH: I want to move on. I really do.

SHAWN: Do you want *me*, Kenneth?

KENNETH: More than anything. You're the only person who understands me. And the fact that you haven't run away screaming is pretty encouraging.

SHAWN: You're frustrating. But fascinating.

KENNETH: And I think you're beautiful. Especially now.

SHAWN: By the light of your computer screen? I'm sure it does wonders for my skin tone.

(KENNETH *turns off the computer.*)

KENNETH: How's that?

SHAWN: Now you can't see me at all.

KENNETH: I like it this way.

SHAWN: I want you to see me.

KENNETH: I know you're there.

SHAWN: Then come and find me.

(*He gets up from his chair and slowly crosses to her. He finds her in the darkness and begins to caress her under her robe.*)

KENNETH: There you are.

SHAWN: She's not dead, you know.

KENNETH: Don't talk about her.

SHAWN: She's alive and well. With a brand new life. And someone new. She's happy without you.

KENNETH: Don't...don't.

SHAWN: I can make you forget all about her.

KENNETH: I know you can.

(She kisses his ear in the darkness, whispering.)

SHAWN: Forget...forget.

KENNETH: I've forgotten everything. I've forgotten my name.

SHAWN: Then I'll give you something to remember.

(She kisses him. They slowly drop to the floor.)

Scene Seven

(The office cubicle, late at night. The only illumination is from the computer screen.)

(CHAD is at the computer, typing.)

(SHAWN and KENNETH remain onstage in silhouette.)

CHAD: "Dear...Sirs...Check...today's...financial...report. Are...you...getting...the...best...return...on...your... investments? A...Concerned...Observer." *(He thinks.)* No. *(He deletes the last part.)* "A...Special...Friend." *(He sends the e-mail.)* Send to the Hawthorne Group. *(He reads the screen prompt.)* Do I want to save? *(He smiles.)* Only love can deliver salvation. *(He hits a button.)* Shut Down.

(Lights out)

END ACT ONE

ACT TWO

Scene Eight

(The Pub at lunchtime. KENNETH, SHAWN and CHAD all share a toast at the table.)

KENNETH: To friendship.

SHAWN: Love.

CHAD: And depravity.

KENNETH: Forever and ever.

SHAWN: Amen.

(They clink glasses. KENNETH and SHAWN follow the toast with a kiss.)

CHAD: Jesus, any excuse.

SHAWN: Kenneth and I have an idea.

CHAD: We can all see that. Why don't you get a room?

SHAWN: We've been talking about you.

KENNETH: Don't frighten the man, Shawn.

SHAWN: Have your ears been burning?

KENNETH: We spent an hour discussing it.

CHAD: Glad to know your tongues can operate independently.

SHAWN: We've decided to make you our new project.

CHAD: Project?

KENNETH: I told her you'd be embarrassed.

SHAWN: We don't want you to be left out. We'd like you to be able to share in the happiness we've found.

CHAD: I'm not into threesomes.

SHAWN: Be serious. We want your permission.

CHAD: For what?

SHAWN: To fix you up.

(Pause)

CHAD: Didn't know I was broken.

SHAWN: You don't have to put on this show for us. We're your friends. We know there's a caring, vulnerable person hiding deep down inside.

CHAD: News flash. He's not hiding. He's *dead*. Been dead for years. Know who did it? The last bitch who dumped him.

KENNETH: That's an ugly word, Chad.

CHAD: What, dumped? I agree.

SHAWN: It's just part of his act. He doesn't mean it.

CHAD: Oh, I mean it all right. I witnessed it. She put a gun to his chest and pulled the trigger. Just so she could watch his heart explode and ooze down his shirt.

KENNETH: There goes my appetite.

CHAD: So Mister Vulnerable died. But I lived on. The freak without a heart.

SHAWN: Don't be defensive, Chad. We just want to help you.

CHAD: What am I, a charity case?

SHAWN: No. Just...romantically challenged. So we've been looking around, and found a very attractive prospect. Vicki in accounting.

CHAD: Vicki.

SHAWN: That's right.

CHAD: Have you mentioned this to her yet?

SHAWN: No. But I notice she has a very physical response whenever you're in the room.

CHAD: Very observant. Do you know why?

SHAWN: Why?

CHAD: She fucking *hates* me. That's why.

SHAWN: And why's that?

CHAD: Because I screwed her for two solid weeks before moving on to the office intern. For some inexplicable reason she took offense.

SHAWN: All this anger. You know it's only because you hurt so much.

CHAD: Interesting theory. Here's another one. What if I'm just really *angry!*

SHAWN: That's the easy version. What you *want* people to think. But I don't believe it for a second.

CHAD: Fine. Whatever. *(To* KENNETH*)* Cat got your tongue? Why aren't you participating in all this head shrinking?

KENNETH: I don't know you well enough.

CHAD: And thank you for that.

SHAWN: Don't get insulted. We'll take Vicki off the list.

CHAD: I want you to take the *list* off the list. Please. Don't help me. It's humiliating.

SHAWN: Why are you so determined to be alone?

CHAD: *(To* KENNETH*)* Speak up, man. What does it take to inspire a little gender loyalty?

SHAWN: He's on my side. Show him, darling.

CHAD: *Et tu*, Kenneth?

KENNETH: It's nothing, really. The best I could do under the circumstances. I'm afraid I don't have much experience when it comes to meeting people...

(KENNETH *hands him a slip of paper, which* CHAD *reads.)*

CHAD: What the hell is this?

KENNETH: Access code to a chat room. On the Internet.

CHAD: Why don't you just kill me? I'm obviously beyond hope.

KENNETH: It's designed for brokers and financial managers. It's called "The Stock Room." Used to be called "Bondage." But too many people didn't get the pun.

CHAD: No thanks.

SHAWN: Give it a try, Chad.

KENNETH: There are some nice people on line. One or two single women, even. They claim to be very attractive.

CHAD: Then I'm sure it's true.

SHAWN: *(to* KENNETH*)* You never told me that part.

KENNETH: What's to tell? We didn't even use our real names.

CHAD: Anonymous fantasies with total strangers. Isn't that why God created phone sex?

KENNETH: No sex, actually. It's just a chat room. For companionship.

CHAD: Know what? Then it's *pointless.*

(He hands the note back to KENNETH.*)*

KENNETH: Probably.

SHAWN: If only you'd make more of an effort. Then we wouldn't have to try so hard.

CHAD: Shawn. I beg you. As a friend. As your special friend. Quit trying. I don't want your help.

KENNETH: I told you, babe.

SHAWN: You were right, sweetheart. I should have listened to you.

KENNETH: You meant well.

SHAWN: Forgive me?

KENNETH: No harm done.

(They kiss.)

CHAD: God, I need a drink.

KENNETH: Buy him a refill, Shawn. The poor guy deserves it after what we just put him through.

(A buzzer goes off in his pocket. He pulls out a Blackberry and checks the text message.)

KENNETH: Sorry, guys. Have to cut lunch short. Another message from the Hawthorne group.

SHAWN: Again?

CHAD: What's the problem?

KENNETH: I'm not sure. They just seem extremely nervous. The slightest fluctuation in the market, and they get itchy.

CHAD: That's how some of them get. It's like reassuring an insecure lover.

SHAWN: Watch it, Chad.

KENNETH: No, he's right. I'm still pretty insecure with this lovely lady. I still can't believe my good luck. It's like a dream.

SHAWN: Wanna pinch me?

CHAD: Allow me.

SHAWN: It's more fun from Kenneth.

KENNETH: Don't tell him *all* our secrets.

CHAD: Why not? Apparently I have no life of my own. Might as well allow me to live vicariously through you.

SHAWN: Don't work too hard today, baby. Save some of that energy for after hours.

(She kisses him goodbye.)

KENNETH: Now's your chance to talk about me while I'm gone.

CHAD: Don't worry, we will.

*(*KENNETH *exits.* SHAWN *watches him go, enraptured.)*

CHAD: Earth to Shawn. Hello?

(He snaps his fingers next to her face.)

SHAWN: I hear you.

CHAD: I don't think you're hearing anything. You're under some kind of bizarre hypnosis.

SHAWN: Just be happy for me, Chad.

CHAD: I'd be glad to. If I could find you. You've been replaced by some mesmerized replicant.

SHAWN: I'm sorry you think so.

CHAD: What other tricks does he make you do? Strip naked in sales meetings while you sing the national anthem? Since when did you become so suggestible?

SHAWN: I know what I'm doing, trust me.

CHAD: Trust you? I don't even *know* you. What have you done with Shawn?

SHAWN: Which Shawn is that?

CHAD: The one with a skeptical eye. The one with an ironic edge.

SHAWN: When I think about the way I used to be... it's like a character in some novel I read long ago.

CHAD: I preferred the writing.

SHAWN: I don't remember that person. And I certainly don't miss her. I'm not even sure she ever existed.

CHAD: Oh, she existed all right. But who am I talking to now?

SHAWN: A woman in love. Does that terrify you?

CHAD: Absolutely. It doesn't suit you.

SHAWN: Who are you to...oh, I get it.

CHAD: Get what?

SHAWN: Why you're taking this so personally. You've got too much invested, don't you?

CHAD: In what?

SHAWN: In me. You're still infatuated.

CHAD: Don't flatter yourself, my dear.

SHAWN: What's the matter, Chad? Did I just find a great big button to push?

CHAD: It's just like you to totally twist my intentions.

SHAWN: So now I'm myself again? Make up your mind.

CHAD: I promised you friendship.

SHAWN: A *special* friendship, as I recall. I'm still unclear on the definition.

CHAD: Then here it is. Being protective. Asking hard questions. Not allowing you to drift thoughtlessly into dangerous territory.

SHAWN: Involving yourself in my personal life.

CHAD: Guilty as charged. Because I don't want to see you get hurt.

(Pause)

SHAWN: All right, I'll bite. Why would I get hurt?

CHAD: Look. I just want you to be happy. I want this thing with Kenneth to work as much as you do. But my only request is that you slow down a little bit. And ask yourself how well you really know this guy. How long have you been together? A few weeks? What do you really know about him? Where he comes from? What he's really doing here? Whether he really loves you?

SHAWN: He says he does.

CHAD: And that's suddenly good enough for you? That's what I'm talking about, Shawn. You once told me you believed in *action*. So what does he do for you? Besides fixing the occasional microwave chicken? Or buying you a rose or two when he passes the blind peddler on the corner?

SHAWN: He does things.

CHAD: Like what? What challenges have you offered him?

SHAWN: He doesn't need to prove his love for me.

CHAD: How else will you know that it's real?

(Pause)

SHAWN: You're confusing me.

CHAD: Look, it's your love affair. What can I possibly know about it?

SHAWN: That's right.

CHAD: I'm sure he's already talked about his plans for the future. So you must know where you fit in.

SHAWN: What do you mean?

CHAD: The future. Where he sees himself in the future. The things he wants from life. Obviously you're confident that his plans include you.

SHAWN: It's too soon to talk about marriage.

CHAD: Who's talking about marriage? I'm talking about a man's personal life track. Every man has one. Like a railroad track.

SHAWN: Life is a railroad. I think this metaphor died with the advent of the horseless carriage.

CHAD: It still applies. Every man sees himself as conductor of his own engine. Sometimes it's supersonic, sometimes it's light rail, sometimes it's weighed down with excess freight. Sometimes with passengers from previous rest stops. And you have to compete for a seat.

SHAWN: You mean "Ursula." Very clever.

CHAD: And sometimes—it's a monorail.

(Pause)

SHAWN: What if...he never talks about the future?

CHAD: Hard to say. But if a man's not sure what track he's on...it may be a runaway train. Someone could get hurt.

(Pause)

SHAWN: What should I do?

CHAD: Just ask a few relevant questions. About where you really fit in the picture. No big deal. If you get the answers you're looking for—then we'll *both* be happy.

SHAWN: You really mean that?

CHAD: Sure. Why would you ask?

SHAWN: I thought maybe... Never mind. I guess I misjudged you.

CHAD: That's okay. Friends forgive, right?

SHAWN: But I still feel bad for you. You deserve love in your life too.

CHAD: No one deserves anything. You have to make things happen.

Scene Nine

(The office cubicle. KENNETH *is on the phone.)*

KENNETH: Yes sir... Yes... Yes. I've seen this morning's market report. But as I explained yesterday...yes sir, but these small variables don't mean that much from day to day. The blue chips have always shown strong progress over the long term, and the mutuals...I promise you it's the most conservative plan we can offer. And still offer a decent return on your portfolio...I wouldn't recommend that, sir. You might as well open a money market account at the local savings and loan... No, that's not a suggestion...

*(*CHAD *enters and sits on the edge of* KENNETH's *desk, waiting for him to finish. He nonchalantly fingers through* KENNETH's *papers.)*

KENNETH: That would be a mistake...I don't believe I am taking a tone, sir. It's just that a little risk is required for a decent return...look— *(He becomes aware of* CHAD *and closes the file folders.)* I'll look through the plan again, try to remove anything that shows short-term instability... You're welcome, sir. Your happiness is our paramount concern. *(He hangs up.)* Moron.

CHAD: The Hawthorne Group?

KENNETH: Someone's been putting ideas in their heads.

CHAD: Who?

KENNETH: Don't know. But it's getting harder and harder to calm their paranoia.

CHAD: You said it yourself, Kenneth. It's a risk-taking business.

KENNETH: Exactly.

CHAD: Some people aren't up to the challenge.

KENNETH: What can I do for you, Chad?

CHAD: Well...this might be a bad time. To talk on a... personal level.

KENNETH: Go ahead.

CHAD: You're sure.

KENNETH: It's okay.

CHAD: As long as you're comfortable. I hope you've come to think of me as a friend.

KENNETH: Of course.

CHAD: I wouldn't blame you if you don't. I was a bit of an asshole at first. When we first met.

KENNETH: I never thought that.

CHAD: Oh, come on. I must have put you off a little.

KENNETH: Well...

CHAD: It's shyness. I get insecure when I meet new people.

KENNETH: I'm the same way.

CHAD: I assume they won't like me. So I confirm their suspicions. It's not very healthy behavior.

KENNETH: Hey, don't worry about it. I know Shawn is a close friend of yours. And that's good enough for me.

CHAD: I'm glad to hear that. I was worried that being around me would make you...uneasy.

KENNETH: Why should it?

CHAD: You know...considering our previous relationship.

KENNETH: I'm not...whose relationship?

CHAD: She didn't tell you?

KENNETH: You and...

CHAD: Oh shit. She never mentioned it? Me and my big mouth.

KENNETH: Shawn and you—

CHAD: Please don't say anything to her. She'd only deny it.

KENNETH: This is...news to me.

CHAD: It's over, man. Long over. We're just good friends. You can see that.

KENNETH: Well...yes...but I never knew...

CHAD: It burned out fast. Too...intense. You know? Nothing can withstand that kind of heat for very long.

KENNETH: I don't know if I should be hearing this...

CHAD: But this is the very thing I need to tell you. You're perfect for her, Kenneth. And she's completely in love with you.

KENNETH: She is?

CHAD: She's ecstatic. Entranced. Exhilarated. I've never seen her like this.

KENNETH: Really? This is so good to hear—especially coming from you.

CHAD: The horse's mouth.

KENNETH: Because—I think I love her too.

CHAD: As you should. Way to go. But...umm...

KENNETH: What?

CHAD: Never mind.

KENNETH: Don't do that, Chad. What is it?

CHAD: You haven't told her yet, have you? About your feelings.

KENNETH: Not yet.

CHAD: Good.

KENNETH: Why is that good?

CHAD: You don't wanna fuck up a good thing.

KENNETH: What are you talking about?

CHAD: She freaks out when men come on too strong. She prefers a long incubation period. So she can get comfortable first.

KENNETH: Comfortable.

CHAD: She values her independence, Kenneth. Hates men who get clingy.

KENNETH: I had no idea.

CHAD: Her major issue, believe me. Don't repeat my mistakes.

KENNETH: What did you do?

CHAD: Me? You kidding? I came on like a bulldozer. Proposed that we see each other exclusively. I'm *still* kicking myself over that little suggestion.

KENNETH: Jesus.

CHAD: If I had known then what I know now—but no, I thought it would be better to share my hopes and desires. What a fool I was.

KENNETH: Desires? Like...what, exactly...

CHAD: Oh, you know, dreams about the future, what our life might be like together, that sort of thing. I thought she'd feel the same way. But she said she wasn't ready. I was putting her in a box. So zoom— out the door in record time.

KENNETH: She's afraid of commitment?

CHAD: Disdainful. To a woman like her, life must be filled with options. But look who I'm telling about Shawn. You must know all this by now.

KENNETH: Not...everything.

CHAD: Good God, man. Glad I caught you before you did some damage.

KENNETH: What should I do?

CHAD: Very simple. Don't stifle her with promises. Let her know she's free to pursue all possibilities.

KENNETH: You mean—other men?

CHAD: It will never happen, believe me. But she'll adore you for giving her the suggestion.

(The desk phone rings.)

CHAD: Food for thought, right? I'll let you get that.

(CHAD playfully punches him on the shoulder as he exits. KENNETH thoughtfully watches him go, then picks up the phone.)

KENNETH: This is Kenneth... You can transfer that here... Hello, Mrs Wharton. So glad you... Well, sure, in my younger years... Eye of the needle. Hmm. Vaguely... Let's see. Something about it being harder for a rich man to enter the kingdom of Heaven than a camel to go through the eye of a needle. Am I close? ...Oh no. I can see why you might think that, but... Hold on now. In the first place, I think you're the last person who needs to worry... Let me finish. And in the second place, notice the Bible says "rich *man*", so you don't have to...no, I wasn't—okay, yes, a little joke. I didn't mean to... Look, if you feel that way, we can make arrangements to donate a small percentage to UNICEF, maybe the Red Cross... *(He stands in horror.)* *How much?*

Scene Ten

(The Pub. KENNETH *sits across from* SHAWN, *who is troubled.)*

SHAWN: I don't understand. Do you have plans?

KENNETH: No. I just thought...you know...if you need the weekend to yourself...I'll understand.

SHAWN: Understand what? We both have two days off. Don't you think we ought to spend them together?

KENNETH: If you want.

SHAWN: Don't you?

KENNETH: Sure. I just don't want to...you know... take up your time. If there's something you'd rather do. I don't want to make any assumptions. You know what I mean.

SHAWN: Not really.

KENNETH: Look. I'm cool...if you are.

SHAWN: Oh. That's clear.

KENNETH: Good.

(He sees CHAD *enter, and waves him over.)*

KENNETH: Look, it's Chad. Over here, buddy!

SHAWN: "Buddy"?

*(*CHAD *sits at their table.)*

CHAD: Not interrupting, I hope?

KENNETH: Not at all. You two could use more time alone anyway. I've got to check on my accounts.

(KENNETH *leans over to kiss* SHAWN. *She offers her lips, but he pecks her on the cheek.* KENNETH *exits.*)

SHAWN: Something's wrong.

CHAD: With what?

SHAWN: He's pulling away. Not as committed as he used to be.

CHAD: Have a little sympathy, Shawn. Don't forget about "Ursula".

SHAWN: Believe me, I haven't.

CHAD: This affair came about awfully fast, you know.

SHAWN: So what?

CHAD: So maybe he's still trying to figure out what he wants.

SHAWN: We should be *beyond* that. He should know exactly what he wants—and he should want *me*.

CHAD: You have high expectations.

SHAWN: I don't have patience for men who are wishy-washy. You're not wishy-washy, are you?

CHAD: Well—yes and no.

SHAWN: Very funny.

CHAD: Look. It's how all men are trained—
to be problem solvers.

SHAWN: I thought they were train conductors.

CHAD: Next chapter. Try to keep up. Men are taught from childhood how to analyze every situation, and explore every conceivable option. But though a man might enjoy solving problems, he's reluctant to *fix* them.

SHAWN: So he creates another problem.

CHAD: Now you're catching on.

SHAWN: Is that what Kenneth is doing with me?

CHAD: Don't panic. You probably just want different things. Happens all the time. That doesn't mean you don't love each other.

SHAWN: But if we want different things...how do we make it work? *(Pause)* No answer. From the man who always has an answer.

CHAD: Not always.

SHAWN: I'm in deep shit, aren't I?

CHAD: All right. This is not an answer, just a suggestion, but...why not try to talk it out with him. Ask him what he really wants from you. Get him to take a stand. If you're not satisfied, then...well, it's up to you. But at least you'll know where things lie.

SHAWN: How did you get so smart about these things?

CHAD: I'm not smart. I've just...learned a few lessons. The hard way.

SHAWN: Your heart really *has* been broken, hasn't it?

CHAD: Let's not talk about that.

SHAWN: I never took that as seriously as I should have. But you kept behaving like—

CHAD: An asshole. I know. It's a defense mechanism. Count on you to see through it.

SHAWN: This is so much better.

CHAD: It is?

SHAWN: You've learned how to express your feelings. All he does is hide them away.

CHAD: Why are you so rough on him? He's just having second thoughts. Perfectly normal.

SHAWN: I don't want our love to *be* normal. Or typical. I want it to be extraordinary.

CHAD: I'm sure he does too.

SHAWN: Then why doesn't he say so?

CHAD: What *does* he say?

SHAWN: Oh, various platitudes. About not wanting to tie me down. Making sure I'm free to "pursue other options".

CHAD: What does that mean? Other men?

SHAWN: I assume so.

CHAD: Well, that seems like a noble attitude.

SHAWN: It seems like a man with one foot out the door. Would you ever say something like that?

CHAD: To someone I loved?

SHAWN: Would you?

CHAD: No. I would tell her that she was mine forever. That I could not conceive of spending sixty seconds without knowing she belonged to me. And me alone. And if another man so much as *touched* her, I'd beat his fucking face in. They'd have to pull me off his bleeding, broken body.

SHAWN: There. See? *That's* romantic.

CHAD: A little extreme, don't you think?

SHAWN: This is what men don't understand. We're not frightened of passion. We *long* for it. Any woman in her right mind would snatch you up.

CHAD: You never did.

SHAWN: I might have...reconsidered. If I knew then what I know now.

CHAD: Well, then. Chalk it up to bad timing.

SHAWN: Maybe.

CHAD: So you'll talk to Kenneth?

SHAWN: I think so.

CHAD: Good. This should resolve things.

Scene Eleven

(KENNETH's den. The room is empty. Then KENNETH quietly enters in his bathrobe. He sits in a chair, troubled.)

(He looks back towards his bedroom, then rises to return. Stopping himself, he paces a little around the room. His eyes rest on the computer terminal.)

(He stealthily sits at his desk and moves the mouse, causing the screen to illuminate.)

(He glances back at the bedroom. Then he punches in a password.)

(As before, he reads the text on his screen as we hear the previous VOICE-OVERS.)

VOICEOVER: (Lonely2) Ishmael!

VOICEOVER: (2Sexy4U) Have you come back to us? Life is so boring without you.

(KENNETH types as he speaks.)

KENNETH: "Just...checking...in."

VOICEOVER: (2Sexy4U) We miss you, Ishmael. You can't imagine the creeps on this line.

VOICEOVER: (Lonely2) She's right. For a change.

VOICEOVER: (2Sexy4U) How's the love life going?

VOICEOVER: *(Lonely2)* Never mind that. Tell him about Ursula!

KENNETH: *(To himself)* Ursula?

VOICEOVER: *(2Sexy4U)* God, I forgot! She's been here, Ishmael. Looking for you!

KENNETH: "Ursula? ...My...Ursula?"

VOICEOVER: *(Lonely2)* The one you kept talking about.

KENNETH: "You're...sure...it's...her?"

VOICEOVER: *(2Sexy4U)* She repeated your story word for word.

VOICEOVER: *(Lonely2)* How she told you she couldn't live without you. And skipped town.

VOICEOVER: *(2Sexy4U)* It made me cry all over again. She still loves you, Ishmael.

VOICEOVER: *(Lonely2)* But we didn't know how to reach you.

VOICEOVER: *(2Sexy4U)* We don't even know your real name.

KENNETH: "How...often...does...she...log...on?"

VOICEOVER: *(Lonely2)* Like clockwork.

VOICEOVER: *(2Sexy4U)* Every night at midnight.

(SHAWN enters from the bedroom in her bathrobe, rubbing her eyes.)

SHAWN: Are we back to this now?

(KENNETH swings around.)

KENNETH: Just catching up on some work. *(He quickly switches on his screen saver.)*

SHAWN: This time of night?

KENNETH: It's the Hawthorne Group. They're keeping me jumping.

SHAWN: You didn't say anything when we went to bed.

KENNETH: I forgot. Woke up with a start and realized I had to prepare for a conference call in the morning.

SHAWN: So you'll be up a while?

KENNETH: I think so. You really should go back to bed. No reason for you to lose sleep.

SHAWN: I wonder.

KENNETH: What?

SHAWN: Are you avoiding me, Kenneth?

KENNETH: What do you mean?

SHAWN: This is how it was in the beginning. When you were afraid of getting too close.

(KENNETH *glances at the clock on his desk.*)

KENNETH: I don't know what you mean.

SHAWN: Why are you looking at the clock? Are you expecting a call or something?

KENNETH: Of course not. I'm just...calculating the amount of work I have to do before morning.

SHAWN: Maybe I should leave.

KENNETH: That's what I said. Go back to bed.

SHAWN: No. Maybe I should go home.

KENNETH: Whatever's easiest for you.

SHAWN: You mean easiest for *you.*

KENNETH: I don't understand—

SHAWN: I need some answers from you, Kenneth.

KENNETH: Like what?

SHAWN: Like what do you want?

KENNETH: Right now?

SHAWN: In this relationship.

KENNETH: I want what you want.

SHAWN: Have you given any thought to the future?

KENNETH: The future? Well...I've been waiting for you to decide.

SHAWN: Decide what?

KENNETH: I don't want to dictate the terms of our relationship. I'll go along with whatever you want. I'm completely flexible.

SHAWN: Flexible.

KENNETH: You have the freedom to do whatever you like. I'll be here whenever you need me.

SHAWN: Don't you need *me*?

KENNETH: Look, it's almost midnight. Maybe this isn't the best time—

SHAWN: When is the best time, Kenneth? Is there ever going to be a time for us?

KENNETH: Sure there is. Whenever you're ready.

SHAWN: I'm ready now.

(KENNETH *glances at the clock again.*)

SHAWN: But you're obviously not.

KENNETH: Why don't we discuss this tomorrow?

SHAWN: I don't think so. *(She turns to go.)* I'll get dressed and go. Wouldn't want to disturb you in the midst of a business transaction. *(She leaves the room.)*

KENNETH: Shawn? Shawn! *(He starts to rise and go after her—but is drawn back to the computer screen. He turns off the screen saver.)*

(The chat room is in mid-conversation as he reads the text.)

VOICEOVER: *(Lonely2)* I tell you, he was just here.

VOICEOVER: *(2Sexy4U)* He's still here. He hasn't left the Stockroom.

VOICEOVER: *(Lonely2)* Maybe he just went to the bathroom or something.

VOICEOVER: *(Ursula)* Obviously he doesn't want to hear from me. I should log off.

(KENNETH types frantically.)

KENNETH: "No! I'm...here."

VOICEOVER: *(Ursula)* Hello?

KENNETH: "Ursula? Is...it...really...you?"

VOICEOVER: *(Ursula)* Yes. I thought I'd never find you again. Once you left Palo Alto.

KENNETH: *(To himself)* Palo Alto. Right! It must be her. *(He types again.)* "You...left...me. Tell...me...your...name. Your...real...name."

VOICEOVER: *(Ursula)* Not yet. We have to start over now.

KENNETH: "All...right. Do...you...remember...my...chat...name." *(Pause)* "Ursula? Are...you...still...there?"

VOICEOVER: *(Ursula)* Trying to think. Was it...Jimmy Stewart?

KENNETH: "Close...enough. It...was... "Scottie" Ferguson. From...*Vertigo.*"

VOICEOVER: *(Ursula)* Of course. "Scottie." I remember.

KENNETH: "Obsessed...and...deluded. By...fantasies."

VOICEOVER: *(Ursula)* But I'm not a fantasy. I'm real.

KENNETH: "I...know...that...now. I'm...so...sorry. For...everything."

VOICEOVER: *(2Sexy4U)* Let's give them their privacy.

VOICEOVER: *(Lonely2)* Forget it. This is why I got broadband.

KENNETH: "If...you...don't...mind?"

VOICEOVER: *(Lonely2)* All right, Ishmael.

VOICEOVER: *(2Sexy4U)* Or "Scottie".

VOICEOVER: *(Lonely2)* Don't keep us in suspense this time. Log on soon.

KENNETH: "I'll ... try."

(Pause)

VOICEOVER: *(Ursula)* I think we're alone now.

(SHAWN enters the room, dressed and carrying her bag.)

(She hesitates, watching him. KENNETH feels her presence behind him and turns around.)

SHAWN: You know, even from this distance I can tell what you're doing. You're not working at all. You're on the fucking internet.

KENNETH: I promised to...help someone. At midnight.

SHAWN: You're the one who needs help, my friend. But not from me. *(She turns to go.)*

KENNETH: Shawn? Wait!

(A door is heard slamming offstage.)

VOICEOVER: *(Ursula)* Hello? Where'd you go?

(KENNETH turns around, reads the screen, and quickly types.)

KENNETH: "Sorry. Had...to...answer...the...phone."

VOICEOVER: *(Ursula)* Is it important? Do you have a girlfriend?

(He thinks about this.)

KENNETH: "Not...at...the...moment."

VOICEOVER: *(Ursula)* Did you read the book I gave you?

KENNETH: "Yes."

VOICEOVER: *(Ursula)* Do you remember the ending? The question Ursula asked Birkin?

KENNETH: "Yes. She...asked...whether...her...love...would...be... enough...to...make...him...happy."

VOICEOVER: *(Ursula)* And he said no.

KENNETH: "That's...not...true...for...me."

VOICEOVER: *(Ursula)* Even after all this time?

KENNETH: "Yes."

VOICEOVER: *(Ursula)* No one knows you the way I do.

KENNETH: "Yes. You...understand."

VOICEOVER: *(Ursula)* You need the distance. To feel safe.

KENNETH: "I...used...to. But...now...I want...to...meet...you."

VOICEOVER: *(Ursula)* Not yet. Let's enjoy this first. We're so good together.

KENNETH: "When...we're...not...together."

VOICEOVER: *(Ursula)* You're sure there's no one else? There must be by now.

KENNETH: "No. No...one..." *(He looks at the door and speaks to himself.)* ...but you. *(He types again.)* "My...real...name...is...Kenneth. What's...yours?"

VOICEOVER: *(Ursula)* Not yet, darling.

KENNETH: "When?"

VOICEOVER: *(Ursula)* Soon. I promise. For now you'll be...my Special Friend.

Scene Twelve

(The Pub. CHAD *tries to calm an angry* SHAWN.*)*

SHAWN: What the hell happened? It was over before it started.

CHAD: Maybe that's the best way. Before anyone gets too hurt.

SHAWN: What does this look like?

CHAD: I know, I know. But any relationship that can't survive more than a few weeks—well, maybe it was never that real.

SHAWN: It sure felt real.

CHAD: Because you wanted it to be real. That doesn't mean it *was* real.

SHAWN: Well, how the fuck am I supposed to know what's real and what isn't? All I can do is rely on words. Words, words, words. Just like before. Nothing ever changes.

CHAD: Some things can.

SHAWN: It's like...love is no more than some kind of... thin electronic impulse. Being transmitted over a cracked, sun-baked cable nibbled on by squirrels. Who knows what kind of garbled message is ever received on the other end? And how it's interpreted? It could even sound like a threat. What's the difference between "I love you" and "I want to destroy you"? No more than a tonal inflection. The words don't even matter.

CHAD: No. They don't. You put your faith in action. Remember?

SHAWN: Action? Don't make me laugh. Have you ever seen how men prove their courage? Bungee jumping. Rappelling. Handgliding. Snowboarding. Anything that involves solitary motion. But committing to a relationship? Now *that's* an extreme sport.

CHAD: Is that what Kenneth wants? To be alone?

SHAWN: No. He's back with "Ursula". Can you believe it?

CHAD: She's here?

SHAWN: He doesn't even know *where* she is. They found each other on the net. Back where they started.

CHAD: Jesus. This is definitely one unhealthy fixation.

SHAWN: I don't get it. I'm warm, fully functioning flesh and blood. I'm reasonably attractive.

CHAD: More than that. So much more.

SHAWN: So why would he prefer the company of some cybernetic *ghost*? He can't touch her, he can't hear her, he can't...he can't...

CHAD: Make love to her.

SHAWN: Exactly. What's the appeal?

CHAD: You said it yourself. What you had was too real for him. He prefers the aesthetic distance of electronic fiction.

SHAWN: What a sick, Orwellian way to spend your Saturday nights.

CHAD: It might work for some people. But you and I have another choice.

SHAWN: Like what.

CHAD: A leap of faith. But this leap is no bungee jump. Because we do it together. Holding hands all the way down. And once we step off that precipice, we won't be pulled back by a rubber cord.

SHAWN: What are you saying, Chad? You want to *date* me?

CHAD: No. I want to possess you. I want to wrap myself around you and keep you from harm for the rest of your earthly days. I want my soul to become entwined with yours, until they are one together. Because I'm completely in love with you. And I always have been.

SHAWN: I don't know what to say.

CHAD: But I do.

SHAWN: I'm...totally thrown. We've been friends...

CHAD: *Special* friends. You asked for the definition. Well, here it is.

SHAWN: What exactly are you suggesting?

CHAD: Well, we could go to a movie, discuss its merits over soft drinks and french fries, and shuffle our feet on the front porch of your house until I give you a good-night peck on the cheek and ask whether I can pick you up next Saturday night. Or we can skip the high school preliminaries and go back to my place to make earth-moving, volcanically passionate love to each other. Right now.

SHAWN: No. *(Pause. She stands up and stares down at him.)* My place.

Scene Thirteen

(The office cubicle. A disheveled KENNETH *sits at the desk, trying in vain to gain access to computer files. His clothes are rumpled, and there is visible stubble on his face.)*

*(*SHAWN *enters and stares at him, dumbfounded.)*

SHAWN: Kenneth?

KENNETH: Hi there.

SHAWN: What are you doing here?

KENNETH: I have to talk to you.

SHAWN: It's been three weeks since anyone's even heard from you. Do you have any idea—

KENNETH: It's good to see you, Shawn. *(Pause)* This is the part where you say it's good to see me too.

SHAWN: Where have you been, Kenneth? Have you been getting any sleep at all? When's the last time you changed those clothes?

KENNETH: Look at you. You're beautiful. So beautiful. How could I leave you?

SHAWN: For "Ursula." Remember?

KENNETH: Ah yes. Ursula. I do remember that. See— I have a lot of memory, Shawn. *(He indicates the computer.)* Maybe even more than this contraption. But mine doesn't work as well. Memories of her... and memories of you. Bzzzt! Short-circuits the brain.

SHAWN: I tried to call you. I was worried about you.

KENNETH: See? That's being real. And you're real. But I don't handle real...real well.

SHAWN: I don't.... Here's what I wanted to say. I hope we can still find a way to be friends.

KENNETH: *Special* friends?

SHAWN: If you like.

KENNETH: Oh, goody. Because a man can never have too many special friends.

SHAWN: What's wrong with you?

KENNETH: It's Ursula.

SHAWN: Let me guess. Not what she was cracked up to be, right? That's the risk you took. You *knew* you took it.

KENNETH: She's gone. Again.

SHAWN: Where?

KENNETH: Who knows? Cyberspace.

SHAWN: Wait a minute. You *still* haven't met her?

KENNETH: Everything was scheduled. Time and place. A sweet little café, like the one she worked at in Berkeley. Romantic décor, nice ambiance, not too crowded, candles on the table. And I waited for her. Sipping on my Sprite. Moved up to light beer. Ended up with a series of double Scotches. The management was very polite. They asked for my car keys, called me a cab. And I went home—alone.

SHAWN: She stood you up?

KENNETH: I've been online for three solid weeks, day and night, trying to find her. But she's gone again. So—I'm yours for the taking.

SHAWN: Kenneth. This is pathetic.

KENNETH: I know it seems a little...indecisive.

SHAWN: The word is psychotic.

KENNETH: Tell me what to say.

SHAWN: There's nothing you can say. It's bad enough being rejected for another woman. But for the *idea* of another woman? Screw you.

KENNETH: She wasn't real.

SHAWN: Well, give the man a cigar. Is that supposed to make me feel better? I don't think this woman was *ever* real, Kenneth. It's all some scheme you've invented. Because if, God help you, things ever start to *get* real, you can always rely on this good old emotional roadblock to keep you from getting too close. You even gave it a name. Like a pet. "Ursula" my ass.

KENNETH: You hate me now.

SHAWN: It's too much *effort* to hate you, Kenneth. I save all my energy for my new lover.

KENNETH: There's someone new?

SHAWN: It's important that you know. So you'll have absolutely no more expectations.

KENNETH: And he...makes you happy?

SHAWN: He tries. At least he has a finer grasp on the things I require. Like honesty. And fidelity. And sanity.

KENNETH: You deserve all that. And more.

SHAWN: There are other women, Kenneth. One of them will be right for you.

KENNETH: No. Only you. I can't live without you.

SHAWN: Those are words, Kenneth. Nothing more. She said them to you, and now you're saying them to me. The last thing that will get my sympathy is recycled sentimentality.

KENNETH: Okay, if it's action you want—then action you'll get.

(He gets off the chair and kneels in front of her on the floor.)

SHAWN: What are you doing?

KENNETH: I'm begging you. Like a fucking dog.
Give me another chance.

SHAWN: Get up from there. People are watching us.

KENNETH: I'm not ashamed.

SHAWN: Well, you should be.

KENNETH: I love you too much.

(He grabs her by the leg and tries to kiss her knee.)

SHAWN: Let go of me this instant. This is *insane.*

KENNETH: Please. I can't lose you too!

(She calls off.)

SHAWN: Chad! Chad, come in here!

(She pulls away from him, letting him sprawl on the floor.)

*(CHAD enters and stares down at KENNETH, who doesn't
bother to get up.)*

CHAD: Jesus Christ.

SHAWN: Keep him away from me. I can't take any more
of this. *(She starts to move off.)*

KENNETH: Shawn. Don't walk away.

*(She hesitates, then turns back and crouches down in front of
him, while CHAD watches.)*

SHAWN: What happened to you, Kenneth? When we
first met, I thought you were the most self-contained
man I ever met. You didn't need anyone at all. Frankly,
that's what attracted me.

KENNETH: I need you.

SHAWN: I guess you do. And I have to say—I'm
disappointed.

(She turns, touches CHAD's *arm lightly in a gesture of thanks, and exits.)*

*(*CHAD *kneels down next to* KENNETH.*)*

CHAD: Come on, pal. Up we go.

KENNETH: Leave me alone.

CHAD: You're interrupting progress, man. Some of us work for a living.

KENNETH: Work.

CHAD: That's right. Work.

KENNETH: There's always work. *(He pulls himself up and sits in the chair, staring at the computer in a daze.)* But I can't get in.

CHAD: Look, she just doesn't... Are you talking about the computer?

KENNETH: My accounts. I can't get into my accounts.

CHAD: Of course not, man. You lost your security clearance.

KENNETH: How come?

CHAD: Kenneth. Surely you're aware that you've been fired.

(Pause)

KENNETH: Aware? No, I haven't been very...aware.

CHAD: Come on, man. You don't show up for three solid weeks, Mrs Wharton's calling us with daily excerpts from the Old Testament, the Hawthorne Group is analyzing *The Wall Street Journal* like it's *The Daily Racing Form*—someone had to step in. And reassure the investors. This is a business. *(He bends down behind the desk and brings up an open carton.)* Here. I took the personal responsibility of emptying your desk. Good thing too. Management just wanted to toss this shit in the dumpster. Strange, but you don't garner much loyalty, Kenneth. Don't know why. Maybe if you tried harder—like, say, a little candy dish on your desk. Always a good idea. Miniature tootsie rolls, toffies, butterscotch— a small gesture of friendliness. It could have made the difference. After all, people are all the same. They just want a little mutual regard. It doesn't take much effort—just a little persuasion. You don't even have to mean it. Anyway, lucky thing I was around when they scraped the name off your door. I said, hold on, let's accord this poor guy a little respect. He'll probably want his calculator back. At the very least.

KENNETH: Thanks.

CHAD: Don't mention it. And don't fret about your old accounts either. I'm handling them personally.

KENNETH: What did you tell them about me?

CHAD: That you have a brain tumor. *(Pause)* Okay with you?

KENNETH: Sure. What the fuck.

CHAD: That's the spirit.

(KENNETH *has been searching the contents of the carton.)*

KENNETH: Something's missing.

CHAD: I took care to save everything. Maybe a few pencils—

KENNETH: A picture. In a frame.

CHAD: Oh. Yes. The picture.

KENNETH: It was sitting on my desk.

CHAD: A picture of Shawn.

KENNETH: It said, "Love you forever".

CHAD: I know. It's perfectly safe.

KENNETH: Where?

CHAD: On *my* desk.

KENNETH: I'd like it back.

CHAD: That's not going to happen.

KENNETH: And why the hell not?

CHAD: She didn't tell you, did she?

KENNETH: Tell me what?

CHAD: About her and me. Her and I. She and I.
I'm not up to speed on my pronouns.

KENNETH: She said she was seeing someone. She didn't
say who.

CHAD: Sparing your feelings, I'm sure. It's always
harder when it's somebody you know.

KENNETH: She gave that picture to me.

CHAD: I didn't see your name on it. I'd say it's a clean
transfer.

KENNETH: It's all I have left to remember her.

CHAD: Then you're better off without it, don't you
think? Time to get a grip and move on.

KENNETH: You said you were my friend. You
convinced me of it.

CHAD: Hard work indeed. Took all of five minutes.

KENNETH: How much betrayal am I expected to endure?

CHAD: Oh, your capacity for that is pretty astonishing.
So take heart. I'm sure you'll find some other special
friend out there.

(Pause)

KENNETH: Special friend?

CHAD: You have your things back. Be sure to leave your forwarding address at the front office. *(He turns to go.)*

KENNETH: "Ursula" used that phrase. On the internet. Special friend.

(CHAD stops and turns back.)

CHAD: And this is significant because...?

KENNETH: I gave you the access code.

CHAD: You're babbling, Kenneth. More than usual.

KENNETH: You used the access code to gain admittance to the chat room.

CHAD: This is delusional. Even for you.

KENNETH: I gave you the code myself.

CHAD: Which I gave right back to you.

KENNETH: After memorizing it.

CHAD: You're one sick puppy, my friend. My strong advice is to seek professional help.

KENNETH: You could have gotten all the info you needed from my files. Like Palo Alto.

CHAD: This is sad.

KENNETH: But how did you figure out my old chat name? Wait a minute—you didn't. I gave it to you. After you said— *(He starts digging into the carton.)*

CHAD: Am I supposed to be following this?

(KENNETH pulls out an old, black and white publicity still—from Vertigo.)

KENNETH: Jimmy Stewart. Tacked to my cubicle. You'd been looking at it for weeks.

CHAD: Kenneth—

KENNETH: That leaves D H Lawrence. How did you— *(He snaps his fingers.)* Shawn told you. Right?

CHAD: Are you done?

KENNETH: You impersonated Ursula.

CHAD: You are seriously unhinged.

KENNETH: The Hawthorne Group—you sent them the anonymous warnings. And Mrs Wharton— the Christian pamphlets. You engineered everything.

CHAD: These are disturbing accusations, Kenneth.

KENNETH: They certainly are. I think I'll have a little talk with Shawn. *(He stands up and begins to leave.)*

CHAD: Go ahead. I'm sure she's forgotten all about your little floor show.

(KENNETH hesitates, turns and looks at CHAD.)

CHAD: What's the matter? Wondering about your credibility?

KENNETH: She'd believe me.

CHAD: Of course she would. It's no crazier than any other theory based on conspiracy and paranoia. And certainly no crazier than crawling around on the floor in front of the entire sales department.

KENNETH: But it's the truth.

CHAD: And I'm sure she'll see how much you want to believe that.

(KENNETH looks off, unable to move.)

CHAD: People can talk themselves into anything, man. But you're the king of suggestibility.

KENNETH: She loved me.

CHAD: Good example. *(He hands him the carton.)* We're gonna miss you, Kenneth. Watching you delude yourself was always a great source of entertainment.

(CHAD exits. KENNETH stands with the carton, somewhat dazed. He turns and looks at the computer. He smiles and presses a button on the keyboard.)

KENNETH: Return.

Scene Fourteen

(The office cubicle.)

(CHAD is alone, typing on the computer keyboard.)

(SHAWN comes up behind him and touches him.)

CHAD: Late for lunch, I know. Just checking my e-mail.

SHAWN: Chad.

(He turns and looks at her.)

SHAWN: We need to talk.

CHAD: Sounds serious.

SHAWN: These last few weeks—after Kenneth—

CHAD: Hey. Don't even bring it up. That shit's behind us.

SHAWN: I agree. And you helped me through the whole thing. You've been so wonderful to me.

CHAD: Why is this all past tense?

SHAWN: Admit it. Things just aren't the same as when we were friends.

CHAD: That's right, they're better. And we're still friends.

SHAWN: I'm glad you think so. That's what I wanted to hear.

CHAD: What's that supposed to...what the fuck is this?

SHAWN: I'm sorry. I didn't want to be another addition to your alphabet.

CHAD: Yeah, yeah. Cut to the chase. Who is he? Who's the guy?

SHAWN: Well, this is the weird part...

CHAD: Kenneth?

SHAWN: Oh God, no. I could never go through that again.

CHAD: I thought he would try.

SHAWN: He did. But you saw what he was like. It got worse. All of these bizarre accusations about you.

CHAD: Me?

SHAWN: At three in the morning, usually. I had to unplug the phone.

CHAD: You didn't believe him.

SHAWN: Of course not.

CHAD: That's a relief. For your sake, I mean. Now who's this other guy?

SHAWN: Like I said...this is the weird part. Especially after the things I said to Kenneth.

CHAD: What?

SHAWN: I met him on the internet.

(Pause)

CHAD: This is a joke, right?

SHAWN: I know it's hard to believe—

CHAD: Tell me this is a joke.

SHAWN: I got curious. I wanted to see what the appeal was. And I'm very lucky. To have found someone so right for me.

CHAD: Oh, right. A man you never even met. Or have you?

SHAWN: Not yet. Neither of us are in a hurry. We're smart enough to know the likelihood of... disappointment.

CHAD: Which will *come*. You *know* it will.

SHAWN: As far as I'm concerned, I don't care if we *ever* meet. And he feels the same way.

CHAD: Listen to what you're saying, Shawn. Do you hear the perversity?

SHAWN: He loves me.

CHAD: And I don't?

SHAWN: It's different with him. It's like he can see into my soul. No one knows me the way he does.

CHAD: Where have I heard...did he say that to you?

SHAWN: His very words. We both need the distance. To feel safe.

CHAD: His words too?

SHAWN: Yes... Why?

CHAD: And he doesn't care if you ever meet....

SHAWN: I think he'd prefer it that way. I don't mind.

CHAD: Shawn. Listen to me. It's Kenneth.

SHAWN: No. His name is Robert.

CHAD: His chat name.

SHAWN: No. His real name. We're way beyond the chat names.

CHAD: You just *think* you are. But I'm telling you it's Kenneth, using a brand new alias. It's no different from "Ishmael."

SHAWN: Who's that?

CHAD: Never mind. Those words from "Robert". About distance. Safety. And knowing you better than you know yourself. The language proves it.

SHAWN: Proves what?

CHAD: It's Kenneth!

SHAWN: You heard him say these things?

CHAD: He never said them! He stole them!

SHAWN: From who?

CHAD: From me!

SHAWN: When was this? *(Pause)* And why?

(Pause)

CHAD: I can explain.

SHAWN: You fucking asshole.

CHAD: Just give me a second...

SHAWN: Like I said—bizarre accusations. But they began to remind me of something.

CHAD: What?

SHAWN: The Chad I used to know.

CHAD: Kenneth wasn't right for you. I proved that beyond a doubt.

SHAWN: And you got all his accounts. Right?

CHAD: It was never about the accounts. It was about you. It was always about you.

SHAWN: Then I hope I was worth it. *(She reaches into an open drawer, and pulls out a running tape recorder.)* Cause you're out of a job.

CHAD: So...there is no Robert.

SHAWN: Of course there's no Robert, dipshit! There's just you and Kenneth and every other creep on this planet who thinks he can manipulate a woman's heart—for the sheer...what...*challenge* of it? Why don't you entertain yourselves some other way?

CHAD: What about you? *All* of you? You never take any responsibility—for any of it! You want to be lied to. So we provide the lies.

SHAWN: Your choice. I can go to management, who might have you arrested for fraud. Or you can empty your desk and get the fuck out of here before anyone notices. I already took my picture off your desk.

CHAD: Right. Your picture. "Love you forever." I suppose you'll be giving that to somebody else— any day now.

SHAWN: Nope. It was contaminated. So I burned it. *(She exits.)*

(We hear the computer sound, indicating new e-mail.)

(We hear the e-mail message in VOICEOVER *as* CHAD *reads the text.)*

(It is the voice of KENNETH.*)*

VOICEOVER: *(*KENNETH*)* Hi, Chad. My name is Ursula. We have a mutual friend. He thought we should get together. Are you free tonight?

CHAD: It's him. *(He frantically types.)* "I...know...who...you...are...you...Kenneth. Game...over." *(He hits the Enter button.)*

(Another computerized VOICEOVER *reflects the pop-up message on his screen.)*

VOICEOVER: *(Computer)* E-MAIL RETURNED. ADDRESSEE DOES NOT EXIST.

CHAD: The hell he doesn't. *(He tries again.)*

VOICEOVER: *(Computer)* DOES NOT EXIST.

*(*CHAD *frantically tries different combinations of keys, but the Voice-over continues to repeat the same cybertext.)*

VOICEOVER: *(Computer)* DOES NOT EXIST. DOES NOT EXIST.

*(*CHAD *stops typing.)*

CHAD: I'll find you, you bastard. So be prepared for the reckoning. *(He hits Enter.)*

VOICEOVER: *(Computer)* ACCESS DENIED.

CHAD: Don't play games with me, fucker! This is REALITY!

(He keeps hitting Enter. Stage lights fade on CHAD *as the computer repeats its message.)*

VOICEOVER: *(Computer)* ACCESS DENIED. ACCESS DENIED. ACCESS DENIED. ACCESS DENIED.

(The stage goes dark.)

END OF PLAY

www.ingramcontent.com/pod-product-compliance
Lightning Source LLC
Chambersburg PA
CBHW052205090426

42741CB00010B/2421